This Book Belongs to:

_____

_____

_____

My First Dictionary

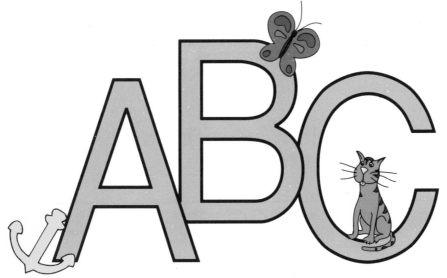

P.S.I. & Associates, Inc.
13322 S.W. 128th Street
Miami, Florida 33186
(305) 255-7959

acorn A seed that grows into a tall oak tree. Many acorns fall from oak limbs.

airport  The place where planes take off and land. There is much activity at the airport.

alligator A long, green reptile that lives near water. Alligators have sharp teeth.

anchor  The hook that keeps a boat from moving. Anchors are very heavy.

ankle A part of the body. Your ankle connects your foot and your leg.

ant A small insect with six legs. Ants work and live in an anthill.

ape A large monkey without a tail. Apes live in the jungles of Africa and Asia.

apple A sweet, crunchy fruit that grows on trees. An apple can be red, yellow or green.

arm The longest part of your upper body. We carry things in our arms.

arrow  A sharp, pointed stick shot from a bow. An arrow shape can show you the way to go.

astronaut A person who travels in outer space. Astronauts ride in space shuttles.

autumn  One of the four seasons of the year. Autumn falls between summer and winter.

baby A very young child. Babies always need love and care.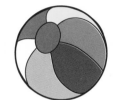

ball 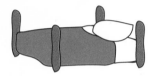 A round toy that can bounce and roll. Many games are played with a ball.

banana A long, yellow fruit that grows in warm places. You peel a banana to get the fruit.

bed A comfortable place to sleep. There is a blanket and pillow on the bed.

bird An animal with wings and feathers. Many birds use their wings to fly.

butterfly  A long, narrow insect with colorful wings. Butterflies grow out of cocoons.

cake A sweet food baked in the oven. Cake and milk are good for dessert.

car  A machine that moves people from place to place. The engine and wheels make the car go.

cat A smart, furry animal. Cats can be big like tigers or small like your pets.

chair A seat for one person. Chairs have a back and four legs.

cheese A useful food made from milk. Cheese is made in many different countries.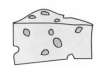

crayon A stick for drawing and coloring. Crayons are made from colored wax.

daisy A flower with white petals and a yellow center. Daisies grow in the spring.

dinosaur A gigantic reptile that lived long ago. Many dinosaurs roamed the earth.

doctor  A person trained to help sick people. Doctors work with nurses.

dog A big or small furry animal you keep as a pet. A baby dog is a puppy.

doll A toy that looks like a person. Soft rag dolls are nice to cuddle.

dress Clothing for a girl. Party dresses have ruffles and bows.

eagle  A large, wild bird from the mountains and forests. Eagles live on mountaintops.

ear A part of your head. We hear sounds with our ears.

egg  A hard-shell food from birds. Chicken eggs are helpful in cooking.

elephant The biggest animal in the jungle. Elephants have long trunks and tusks.

engine  A machine that makes some things move. An engine needs oil and gas to run.

eye A part of your face. We see all there is to see with our eyes.

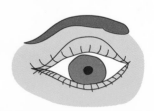

face
The front of your head. My smile, nose and eyes are on my face.

farm

Land where food grows. The farmer has animals on his farm.

flower
A colorful plant that grows from a seed. A flower is very pretty.

foot
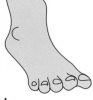
The part of your body at the bottom of your leg. We stand and walk on our feet.

forest
Land where trees and plants grow. Forests help protect the air we breathe.

fox

A wild animal in the forest. The fox has a pointed nose and bushy tail.

gate
A small door in a fence or wall. Gates swing open and closed.

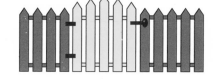

giraffe

The tallest animal in the world. The giraffe has a long neck and legs.

glass
A container for a drink. You can see through glass to find out what you are drinking.

goat
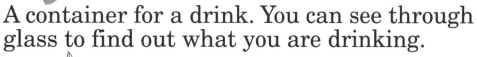
A farm animal with a horn and a beard. Wild goats live in the mountains.

grapes
Small, round fruits that grow on vines. Raisins are made from grapes.

grasshopper
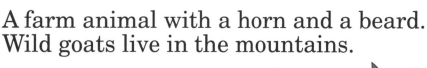
A hopping insect with very long back legs. Grasshoppers eat plants.

hair   A soft covering on your head and arms. Most of your hair is on top of your head.

hat  A cover for your head. Hats protect you from the rain and sun.

heart   An important muscle in your chest. Your heart pumps blood through your body.

horn  A musical instrument shaped like a cone. Blowing a horn makes a loud noise.

horse   A large, strong animal with four legs. Horses can pull heavy wagons.

house  A place where people live. There are many rooms in a house.

ice   Water that is frozen. In winter, rivers and ponds freeze into ice.

icing  The sweet topping on a cake. Cakes are decorated with icing.

igloo   A house made of ice and snow. Eskimos build igloos in Alaska.

ink  The colored liquid inside a pen. Most pens have black or blue ink.

insect   A tiny animal with six legs. There are three parts to an insect's body.

island  Land with water all around it. Islands can be big or small.

10

jacket A short coat to wear in chilly weather. Your jacket has two pockets.

jaguar 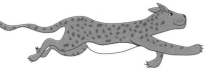 A big, wild jungle cat. There are dark spots on the jaguar's fur.

jam A sweet food made from fruit and sugar. Jam tastes good on peanut butter sandwiches.

jeans  Strong pants made from cotton. We put jeans on when we go out to play.

judge The person in charge of a court. A judge's decisions are guided by the law.

juice  A drink made from fruits. Orange juice is made by squeezing oranges.

kangaroo A large, jumping animal from Australia. The kangaroo carries its baby in a pouch.

king  A man who rules a country. Long ago, kings were very powerful.

kitchen The room in a house where food is cooked. The sink and microwave are in the kitchen.

kite  A toy made to fly in the breeze. Hold the string or the kite will blow away.

kitten A playful, baby cat. Little kittens like to play with string.

koala  An animal that looks like a little bear. Koalas live in the trees of Australia.

lamb A baby sheep that is raised on a farm. Lambs like to eat grass.

leaf  The flat, green part of a plant. In autumn, most leaves change colors.

leg The longest part of the body. Your knee is in the middle of your leg.

lemon  A yellow, sour-tasting fruit. Lemonade is a drink made from lemons and sugar.

letter One part of the alphabet. There are 26 letters in the alphabet for you to learn.

limb  The large branch of a tree. Smaller branches grow from each limb.

lion A large, wild jungle cat of Africa. The roar of a lion is very loud.

lips  The skin around your mouth. Lips help us to pronounce words.

lizard A small reptile with scaly skin and a long tail. Lizards live in the desert.

lock  A piece of metal that keeps things closed. You open a lock with a key.

log Wood from a tree that has been cut down. We burn logs in a fireplace.

lunch  The second meal of the day. Most children eat lunch at school.

map   A picture that shows where places are. Maps can be of a city, state or country.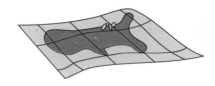

mask A cover worn over a face. On Halloween, children dress up in costumes and masks.

milk   The white liquid that comes from cows and goats. Milk is very healthy to drink.

mittens  A glove with two pouches for the thumb and fingers. Mittens keep your hands warm.

monkey   A small, tree-climbing jungle animal. Monkeys have long tails.

moon  A round, bright object in the night sky. The moon moves around the earth.

mouse   A small, squeaky animal with a long tail. Mice can be pests in the house.

muffler  A heavy scarf that protects your neck. Mufflers are good winter clothing.

mug   A big drinking cup with a handle. A mug makes it easy to drink hot chocolate.

muscle  Parts of the body that help you move. There are muscles everywhere in your body.

mushroom   A plant shaped like an umbrella. Mushrooms grow in dark, wet places.

music   Different sounds that make one awesome sound. People use instruments to make music.

nail A sharp, pointed piece of metal. Nails hold pieces of wood together.

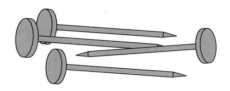

necklace  Jewelry to wear around the neck. Mom likes to wear her gold necklace.

nest A bird's home. Birds use twigs and grass to build a nest.

nose The part of your face that sticks out. You use your nose to smell and breathe.

nurse A person trained to help doctors and sick people. Nurses work in hospitals.

nut  A seed with a hard shell. We use a nutcracker to open nuts.

ocean A large body of salt water. There are five oceans that cover most of the earth.

octopus  A round, sea animal with eight legs. An octopus has suckers on each leg.

orange A round fruit with thick skin. Oranges have tasty sections inside.

orangutan An ape with long, red hair and no tail. Orangutans have long arms.

organ A musical instrument that looks like a piano. Organs make sounds through pipes.

owl  A night-flying bird with a big head and beak. Owls see very well at night.

paint A colored liquid for artwork. You put paint on with a brush.

palace  The home of a king and queen. In olden times, palaces were important places.

pelican  A large bird that lives close to water. Pelicans catch fish in their large beaks.

pencil  A tool for drawing and writing. Pencils are made with graphite and wood.

pig A farm animal with a snout for a nose. Pigs have fat bodies and curly tails.

pocket  A place to hold things in your clothes. There are pockets in your pants.

pony A small horse. Children like to ride ponies.

quail  A plump, brown bird with a short tail. There are many quail in the woods.

quarter One of four parts of a whole. There are four quarters in a dollar.

queen  A woman who rules a country. History tells all about queens.

quill A long feather with a hard stem. Long ago, people wrote with quills.
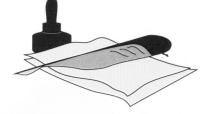

quilt  A thick, homemade blanket. Quilts are decorated in many different ways.

rabbit   A furry animal with long ears. Rabbits like to eat carrots.

reptile  An animal that moves on its tummy or on tiny legs. Turtles, alligators and lizards are reptiles.

rhinoceros   A large animal with thick skin and a horn on its nose. The rhinoceros comes from Africa.

rope   Twisted pieces of string. Rope can be very strong in order to hold heavy things.

rose   A colorful, pretty flower. A rose smells nice, but be careful of its thorns.

ruler  A flat stick used to measure things. You can draw a straight line with a ruler.

scarf   A long piece of cloth. A scarf keeps your neck warm in cold weather.

shrimp 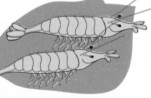 A small sea animal often used as food. Fishermen catch shrimp in their nets.

soup   A watery food made with meat, fish or vegetables. Use a spoon to eat hot soup.

spring  The season of the year when flowers grow. Spring is between winter and summer.

star   A tiny light in the night sky. Many stars appear to twinkle in the dark.

summer  The hot-weather season of the year. Summer is between spring and autumn.

tear A drop of water from your eye. There are many tears when we cry.

teaspoon  A small spoon to eat with. Teaspoons are used to measure food.

throat The inside of your neck. Your throat starts at the back of your mouth.

thunder  The loud sound from the skies made by a storm. Thunder always follows lightning.

tiger A large, wild jungle cat. Tigers have orange and white fur with black stripes.

toast  A slice of warmed bread. Toast is a good way to start to make a sandwich.

tomato A juicy, red fruit with seeds. Tomatoes taste very good in salads.

towel  A cloth to dry people and things with. Towels are made from cotton.

train A row of railroad cars joined together. The wheels of a train roll on a track.

trunk  A large box with a top that closes. Trunks are a good place to keep your toys.

tulip A flower grown from a bulb. Tulips have large petals and bloom in the spring.

turkey A large farm bird with a fleshy neck. Turkey is a favorite food at Thanksgiving.

umbrella Something to protect you from rain. Umbrellas can open and close.

umpire  A person who makes decisions in games. Umpires help teams play fairly.

underwear Clothing worn next to the skin. We wear clean underwear every day.

unicorn  A pretend animal from ancient legends. A unicorn looks like a horse with a horn on its head.

uniform Special clothing worn for a job or by a team. A policeman wears a uniform.

urn  A pretty jar with a special shape. There are many old urns in museums.

valentine A special card to celebrate St. Valentine's Day. You send valentines on February 14.

vase   A long container for flowers. There are roses in the pretty vase.

vegetable Healthy food that grows from a plant. Carrots and radishes are vegetables.

village  A small town far away from big cities. Villages have only a few houses.

vine A climbing plant that grows up walls. Grapes grow on a vine.

violin  A musical instument with strings. You play the violin with a bow.

wagon   A cart with four wheels and a handle. Long ago, horses pulled wagons.

walrus    A large sea animal from the North Pole. A walrus has two long teeth called tusks.

watermelon   A large, sweet fruit with a thick skin. Watermelon is very juicy.

whale   The largest sea animal on earth. Whales breathe air.

wheel   A round object that makes things move. Bicycles, cars, and trains have wheels.

whistle 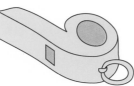   A small, loud instrument. Whistles make shrieking noises.

window   An opening in a wall that lets in light and air. Windows can have glass panes.

winter    The coldest season of the year. Winter is between autumn and spring.

wolf   A wild animal that looks like a dog. Wolves live in forests and mountains.

wool   Sheep or lamb's fur. Wool is used to make warm clothing.

worm   A long thin slippery animal. Worms crawl through the dirt.

wrist    A part of the body. The wrist joins the hand and arm together.

XxYyZz

x-ray — A picture of the inside of your body. An x-ray shows your bones.

xylophone — A musical instrument with bars. You hit the bars with a hammer for the sound.

yak — A large, hairy animal that looks like an ox. Yaks come from Asia.

yard — The land around a house. The back yard is a great place to play.

yarn — Long, thin thread made from wool. You use yarn to knit sweaters.

year — A measure of time. There are 365 days in a year.

yellow — A very bright color. Lemons, the sun, and bananas are all yellow.

yo-yo — A round, spinning toy with a string. Yo-yos spin up and down.

zebra — An African animal like a horse. Zebras have black and white stripes.

zero — One of the ten single numbers. Zero means nothing.

3 2 1 0

zipper — A way to join two pieces of cloth. Zippers make it easy to get dressed.

zoo — A place where animals are kept. People visit zoos to learn about animals.

My First Dictionary Words

acorn	goat	mouse	thunder
airport	grapes	muffler	tiger
alligator	grasshopper	mug	toast
anchor	hair	muscle	tomato
ankle	hat	mushroom	towel
ant	heart	music	train
ape	horn	nail	trunk
apple	horse	necklace	tulip
arm	house	nest	turkey
arrow	ice	nose	umbrella
astronaut	icing	nurse	umpire
autumn	igloo	nut	underwear
baby	ink	ocean	unicorn
ball	insect	octopus	uniform
banana	island	orange	urn
bed	jacket	orangutan	valentine
bird	jaguar	organ	vase
butterfly	jam	owl	vegetable
cake	jeans	paint	village
car	judge	palace	vine
cat	juice	pelican	violin
chair	kangaroo	pencil	wagon
cheese	king	pig	walrus
crayon	kitchen	pocket	watermelon
daisy	kite	pony	whale
dinosaur	kitten	quail	wheel
doctor	koala	quarter	whistle
dog	lamb	queen	window
doll	leaf	quill	winter
dress	leg	quilt	wolf
eagle	lemon	rabbit	wool
ear	letter	reptile	worm
egg	limb	rhinoceros	wrist
elephant	lion	rope	x-ray
engine	lips	rose	xylophone
eye	lizard	ruler	yak
face	lock	scarf	yard
farm	log	shrimp	yarn
flower	lunch	soup	year
foot	map	spring	yellow
forest	mask	star	yo-yo
fox	milk	summer	zebra
gate	mittens	tear	zero
giraffe	monkey	teaspoon	zipper
glass	moon	throat	zoo